6/0

Wetlands Explorer

Mary Quigley

Chicago, Illinois

Editorial: Marta Segal Block/Jennifer Huston
Photo research by Bill Broyles
Production: Sal d'Amico
Map: Guy Holt, Daniel Block
Printed and bound in China by Wing King Tong.

09 08 07 06 05
10 9 8 7 6 5 4 3 2 1

Library of Congress Cataloging-in-Publication Data:
Quigley, Mary, 1963-
  Wetlands explorer / Mary Quigley.
    p. cm. -- (Habitat explorer)
Includes bibliographical references (p.   ).
Contents: Little Islands -- Mangroves -- Manatees.
  ISBN 1-4109-0514-4 (lib. bdg. : hardcover)
      1-4109-0842-9 (paperback)
  1. Wetland ecology--Florida--Everglades--Juvenile
literature. 2.Everglades (Fla.)--Juvenile literature. [1.
Wetlands. 2. Wetland ecology. 3. Ecology. 4.
Everglades (Fla.)] I. Title. II. Series.
  QH105.F6Q55 2004
  577.68'09759'39--dc22
                              2003017126

Acknowledgments
The publisher would like to thank the following
for permission to reproduce photographs:
Title page, icons, pp. 6, 9, 29 PhotoDisc/Getty Images;
pp. 5, 27 Jeff Foott/DRK Photo; p. 7 John Eastcott and
Yva Momatiok/DRK Photo; pp. 8, 15 Lynn M.
Stone/DRK Photo; p. 10 C. C. Lockwood/DRK Photo;
p. 11 John Cancalosi/DRK Photo; p. 12 M. P. Kahl/DRK
Photo; p. 13 Digital Vision/Getty Images; p. 14 Marty
Cordano/DRK Photo; p. 16 John Gerlach/DRK Photo;
p. 17 Tom & Pat Leeson/DRK Photo; p. 18 Stephen G.
Maka/DRK Photo; p. 19 Marc Epstein/DRK Photo; p.
20 George J. Sanker/DRK Photo; p. 21 Stephen J.
Krasemann/DRK Photo; pp. 22, 23, 24 Doug
Perrine/DRK Photo; p. 25 Dan Burton/Nature Picture
Library; p. 26 Webistan Reza/Corbis; p. 28 James A.
Sugar/Corbis

Cover photograph by Robin Prange/Corbis

Every attempt has been made to trace and
acknowledge copyright. Where an attempt has been
unsuccessful, the publisher would be pleased to hear
from the copyright owner so any omission or
error can be rectified.

Contents

The Florida Everglades 4

Out of the Sea 6

A River of Surprises 8

Little Islands 10

The River of Grass 12

Pinelands at Night 14

Day in the Pinelands 16

Coastal Prairie 18

Mangroves 20

Marine Animals 22

Manatees 24

The World's Wetlands 26

The Wetlands' Future 28

Find Out for Yourself 30

Glossary 31

Index 32

Any words appearing in the main text in bold, **like this,** are explained in the glossary.

The Florida Everglades

Imagine you are in a canoe at the edge of Lake Okeechobee in Florida. You have come in the summer wet season. Though the lake is large, it can only hold so much rainwater. The water spills over and moves slowly southward. Tall sawgrass with prickly edges that can cut you grows all around. Welcome to the Florida Everglades.

This map shows the locations of some of the world's many wetlands.

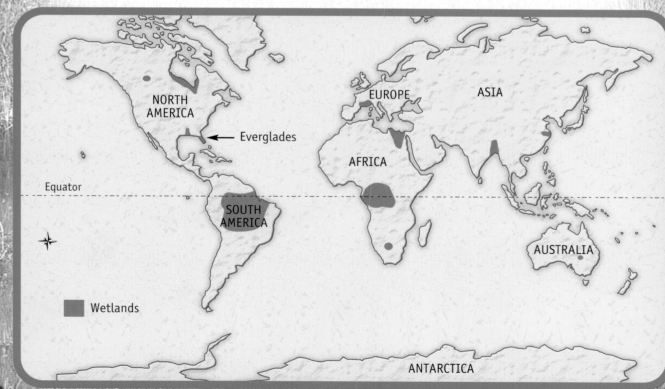

Wetland habitats

The Florida Everglades are wetlands.
There are many different kinds of
wetlands in the world. What they all
have in common is a lot of water. Sometimes the water
is shallow enough to wade in and sometimes it is deeper.
In certain seasons and weather conditions, the water
might even dry up. There are many kinds of **habitats,**
or places to live, in the Everglades.

The sharp edges of sawgrass can make it difficult to travel through the Florida Everglades.

Out of the Sea

Florida used to be covered by ocean. Layers of seashell, sand, and soil piled up. When the water level dropped, the **peninsula** of Florida appeared. The land here is like a sponge. It stores water for dry seasons and clears out **pollutants.**

Explorer's notes

Adaptation: plants and animals can change in response to their surroundings

In the Florida Everglades there is a lot of water you can see. There is also a lot of water under the ground.

6

A tree is growing up and out of the water. Not all trees can do this, but a cypress can. Cypress trees grow a wide base to secure themselves to the ground. Their roots grow up out of the water and form cypress "knees" that let the roots get more air. Cypress trees are well **adapted** to their **habitat.**

Lending a limb

Air plants like to grow on cypress trees. Ferns, moss, and orchids grab a limb, too. They like to be up out of the water. They do not harm the tree. The strangler fig, on the other hand, can kill the tree that it grows on.

Here you can see the "knees" of the cypress tree poking out of the water. The knees provide the roots with air.

A River of Surprises

Some wetland animals are **camouflaged,** or hidden. You might not see the frog sitting very still and watching for insects among the lily pads. You also might not see the alligator watching you, with just the top of its head above the water. All the animals are looking for a meal. Animals that eat other animals are called **predators.** The animals that they eat are called **prey.**

Helping hand

Turtles lay eggs in alligator holes. When animals and plants help each other exist it is known as **interdependence.**

Alligators sometimes eat turtles, but they can also live peacefully together.

Alligators

Explorer's notes

Predator animals hunt; prey animals are the ones hunted. Most animals are both predators and prey.

Alligators don't eat every animal in sight. In fact, they help some animals. Alligators dig holes with their snout and feet to create a place to keep themselves cool. These holes help collect rainwater. Sometimes the alligators find more water underground. The dug-up dirt forms mounds that can become islands where trees and other plants grow. Many animals survive the dry season because of the hard work of the alligators.

This water looks still, but it is really filled with life.

Little Islands

You bring your canoe up to the edge of a small island of trees called a **hammock.** This hammock may have formed on top of the discarded dirt from alligator holes. These teardrop-shaped islands are scattered throughout the Everglades. A natural, watery border around the island, called a moat, protects it from fires in the dry season.

Explorer's notes

Animals seen on the hammock:
- cardinals
- barred owls
- bobcats
- white-tailed deer
- green anoles
- mice
- Everglades racer snakes
- opossums
- raccoons

This hammock island is in a wetland in Louisiana.

Island life

Mice, snakes, birds, raccoons, opossums, and bobcats live here. Wild papaya and custard apples grow on the island.

Animal variety

Not all wetlands have the same plants and animals. Alligators, for instance, would not be found in a cranberry **bog**. The Everglades have some plants and animals that are very rare and need the warm, moist weather of a place like Florida. Some animals, like frogs, can be found in most wetlands, but not always the same **species,** or kind, of frog.

You see a green anole scurrying along a tree trunk. An anole is a small lizard that can change color when frightened. Its oversized toes help it climb trees.

This green anole is just one of the many animals living on the hammock.

11

The River of Grass

You get in your canoe and travel further south. You cut through patches of water lilies. Their large, flat leaves rest on the surface of the water and white flowers bloom. Dragonflies zip and hang in the air like helicopters. Frogs splash when the canoe approaches. There are wading birds such as herons. Songbirds swoop near your canoe. A snail kite, which is a type of hawk, swoops down to snatch an apple snail that has come out of the water for air.

A snail kite's beak is the perfect tool for eating snails.

Explorer's notes

Like people, animals have certain foods that they need to eat to be healthy.

Bird food

The apple snail is the only food that the snail kite likes to eat. This kite has a special **adaptation** for doing that. The beak is shaped like a hook for pulling the snail right out of the unbroken shell. You can tell what a bird eats by looking at the design of the beak. Birds that eat seeds need nut-cracking beaks. Some birds have beaks like spoons for scooping food up out of water. Other birds have beaks that work like spears for catching fish.

Frogs and other wetland animals help control the insect population by eating them.

Pinelands at Night

You hike through tall grasses, heading southeast, toward the pinelands. This area is not wet, but it is part of this wetland **habitat.** Frequent fires destroy trees such as oak and maple, but pines grow well here. The ground beneath the pines is soft with a thick layer of fallen needles. You see a shallow dent where a deer slept. Cones hang from the upper branches. Eventually they will open and release seeds that will begin to grow new pine trees.

Pines stand up to fire

The bark of pines in the Everglades has many layers. If there is a fire, the outer bark will be burned but the inner bark is protected and the tree will continue to grow.

Lightning often starts fires in the drier land of the pinelands.

Scientists use special collars to help keep track of the **endangered** Florida panther population.

Nocturnal animals

As the sun sets, the animals that are awake during the day begin to find places to sleep. Animals that are awake during the night become more active. They are **nocturnal.** You hear the barred owl hooting before the evening hunt. Listen carefully for the panther. This animal is very rare, so you probably will not see one tonight.

Explorer's notes

Only about 30-50 panthers are known to live in the Everglades.

Day in the Pinelands

By morning the raccoons have gone back to sleep but other animals are waking up and making noise. Songbirds have been up since sunrise. Deer are nibbling on plants as they turn their ears to listen to your footsteps. Animals that are awake during the day are **diurnal.**

Rare flowers

Orchids are rare flowers. People often steal them from their **habitats.** There are many kinds of orchids. Vanilla, which is used for flavoring, comes from the pod of a certain orchid.

Orchids that are stolen from their natural habitats often do not grow.

This deer can eat and listen for trouble at the same time.

Fabulous flowers

With the sun up you notice the orchids that you did not see last night. There are many kinds of orchids throughout the Everglades. These flowers are rare because people often steal them.

Explorer's notes

Nocturnal animals are awake at night.

Diurnal animals are awake during the day.

17

Coastal Prairie

You have now traveled 80 miles (129 kilometers). You reach a dry area that is like a desert. You are closer to the ocean and the soil contains more salt. The plants that grow here are desert plants that can live in this type of soil. **Succulents** with thick waxy leaves survive by letting their leaves plump up with water when it rains. Then they have stored water for dry times. Plants may go a long time without water because the water spilling from Lake Okeechobee has been soaked up

Cactus leaves hold a lot of water in between rain storms.

Explorer's notes

Plants of the coastal prairie have waxy leaves that hold in moisture.

by the ground before it gets this far. It has also **evaporated**. Water is only a trickle in some places.

Hurricanes

Hurricanes can hit the Everglades in summer and fall. A hurricane is a tropical storm that is caused when strong winds create large waves on the ocean. The winds swirl wildly because of cold air meeting warm air. The resulting rain and waves may travel inland and cause flooding.

This hurricane hit Florida in 1999.

Mangroves

As you hike further south, the land gets watery again. But the water smells different. It is salty because the ocean mixes with the freshwater here. You have arrived in the mangroves. The mangroves are found along the channels at the southern tip of Florida.

The red mangrove tree

The red mangrove tree has a stilt-like root system. The stilts catch sticks and

The anhinga catches fish with its spear-like beak.

other waste and help form land beneath. They also keep the tree out of the water. When leaves drop into the

Growing seeds

The mangroves do not drop their seeds until they have already sprouted. Salt water prevents seeds from sprouting. By waiting until the seeds have sprouted, the mangrove tree is giving the seedling a better chance of growing.

water they become part of the food chain right away. They are eaten by fish and other animals. You can see an anhinga, which is also called a snake bird. This bird puts its whole body under water and leaves just its neck and head sticking out. When the anhinga does this it looks like a snake.

Mangrove tree roots provide nesting and hiding places for small wetland animals.

21

Marine Animals

You have now arrived in Florida Bay. The marine **estuaries** are channels where seawater travels inland. They are home to coral and sponges. You switch to a larger boat to go out into the bay. A brown pelican carries a load of fish in its beak. A roseate spoonbill wades near the shore and picks through the water with a spoon-like beak. Baby sea turtles that hatch out of a sandy nest on the shore will go out into the bay, too.

Explorer's notes

Sea turtles find their way to the ocean by following the moon.

After they hatch, baby sea turtles make their way back to the ocean.

22

A dolphin can jump high out of the water.

Dolphins

You see dolphins jumping out of the water. Though dolphins live in the water, they are **mammals,** like people. Dolphins live in the ocean but they need to breathe air. They come up to the surface to breathe. They take in air through the blowhole on the top of their head. When they exhale, it is so powerful that it blows most of the water away. This creates an air bubble in which they can breathe. Many people who work with dolphins feel that dolphins are very smart.

Manatees

You see a manatee out in the water. Like dolphins, manatees are also **mammals.** Just like a cow, a manatee grazes on plants. Manatees eat for up to eight hours a day. This helps keep the waterway clear of plants, which is healthy for the Florida Bay.

Explorer's notes

Mammals that live in water:
- dolphins
- porpoises
- whales
- manatees

Manatees can hold their breath for up to 20 minutes under water.

Manatees can eat up to 100 pounds of plants in a day.

Manatees are grayish-brown with front flippers they use for steering in the water and sweeping plants into their mouth. A large lip helps them pull sea plants into their mouth. They can weigh 1,000 pounds (454 kilograms). Because they graze for food, manatees are also called "sea cows." The tail of a manatee is paddle-shaped. This helps the manatee swim. Boaters have to be careful here, because many manatees are hit by boats in the shallow water.

Manatee moms

Manatees use many senses including sound, sight, taste, touch, and smell to communicate with other manatees. A mother manatee makes underwater sounds to keep track of her calf.

The World's Wetlands

You can find wetlands all over the world. Although the Florida Everglades are very big, some other wetlands are small areas inside other kinds of **habitats.** Some wetlands are as big as an entire country. In some wetlands you may not know the ground is wet until you try to step on it.

Egypt

The **delta** of the River Nile is about the same size as the Florida Everglades. People have been growing crops there for thousands of years. In 1970 a dam was completed to control the Nile's floods. This dam helps people who live here, but it may ruin the wetlands of the delta.

This papyrus farm is located in the Nile Delta.

In others the whole area is under shallow water. Swamps, **marshes,** and **bogs** are all different kinds of wetlands. Wetlands often form near rivers, lakes, and oceans. Only rain forests have more kinds of animals in them than wetlands.

Explorer's notes

The word everglade means a grassland covered with water. The Florida Everglades are famous for their grass-filled rivers.

The Everglades National Park is a large part of the Florida Everglades.

27

People have not always understood the beauty of wetlands. In some places they tried to dry them out so the land could be used for homes and businesses. They redirected the flow of water to places where it was needed. It seemed like a way to make the land better. Instead, many plants and animals died. Chemicals have gotten into wetlands, killing plants and animals. New **species** have been

Explorer's notes

Threats to wetlands:
- pollution
- re-directing waterways
- non-native species of plants and animals
- building of cities
- stealing and harming of plants and animals

These children are learning to care for the Florida Everglades.

28

introduced to the wetlands and sometimes they force out the **native** plants and animals.

Saving the wetlands

Wetlands are not only important to animals, they are also an important source of food for people. Today people are working hard to make places like the Everglades healthy again. A large part of the Everglades has been set aside as a national park, which means that the United States government protects it.

Many wetlands are clogged with garbage.

Find Out for Yourself

There are many kinds of wetlands in the world. Check out the kinds of wetlands near you. Even a small wetland can be full of interesting life. Bring a sketchbook and draw the insects, birds, animals, and plants that you find. Then look them up in a field guide to learn more.

Explore the Internet to find out more about wetlands. Websites can change, so if the link below no longer works, use a kid-friendly search engine, such as www.yahooligans.com or www.internet4kids.com, and type in keywords such as "wetland animals" or even better, the name of a particular animal.

Website

www.nps.gov/ever/index.htm
The National Park Service's guide to the Florida Everglades contains helpful information and fun activities.

Books to Read

Bright, Michael. *Endangered and Extinct Animals of the Rivers, Lakes, and Wetlands*. Brooklyn, N.Y.: Millbrook Press, 2002.

Richardson, Adele D. *Wetlands*. Mankato, Minn.: Capstone, 2001.

Stille, Darlene R. *Wetlands*. Danbury, Conn.: Scholastic, 2000.

Glossary

adapt/adaptation how an animal or plant adjusts to its habitat

bog wet spongy ground found next to a body of water

camouflaged blended in with surroundings

delta triangle-shaped land at the mouth of a river

diurnal active during the day

endangered group of animals that are dying out so there are few left

estuary mouth of a river or place where ocean meets freshwater

evaporated when a liquid becomes a vapor and is absorbed by the air

habitat place where a plant or animal lives

hammock small Everglades island

interdependence term used to describe two or more living beings that depend on each other for survival

mammal warm-blooded animal, with at least some hair or fur, that gives birth to young who drink milk from their mother

marsh soft, wet land with grasses and plants

native originally from a place or belonging to a place

nocturnal active at night

peninsula land form that is surrounded by water on three sides and connected to land on the fourth side

pollutant something that causes pollution

predators animal that hunts others for food

prey animal that is hunted by predators to be food

species group of plants or animals that has the same name even though they are not exactly alike

succulent type of plant that can hold a lot of water in its leaves

Index

adaptation 6, 7, 13
alligators . . .8, 9, 10, 11
anoles 11
apple snails 12, 13

beaks 12, 13
birds 11, 12, 13,
  16, 21, 22
bogs 5, 6, 11, 27

camouflage 8

dolphins 23

estuaries 22

frogs 8, 11, 12, 13

habitats 5, 7
hammocks 10, 11
hurricanes 19

Lake Okeechobee . .4, 18

manatees 24–25
mangroves 20–21
marshes 5, 27

Nile Delta 26

orchids 7, 16, 17

panthers 15
pinelands . .14–15, 16–17
pollutants 6, 29
predators 8, 9
prey 8, 9

Ramsar sites 29

sawgrass 4, 5
snail kites 12, 13
succulents 18
swamps 5, 27

trees 7, 9, 14, 20
turtles 8, 22